100 facts

Saving the Earth

First published in 2008 by Miles Kelly Publishing Ltd
Harding's Barn, Bardfield End Green, Thaxted, Essex, CM6 3PX

This edition updated 2018, printed 2019

2 4 6 8 10 9 7 5 3 1

Publishing Director Belinda Gallagher
Creative Director Jo Cowan
Assistant Editor Carly Blake
Volume Designers Simon Lee, Elaine Wilkinson
Cover Designer Simon Lee
Indexer Gill Lee
Image Manager Liberty Newton
Production Elizabeth Collins, Jennifer Brunwin-Jones
Reprographics Stephan Davis, Callum Ratcliffe-Bingham
Assets Lorraine King

ISBN 978-1-78989-145-4

Printed in China

British Library Cataloging-in-Publication Data
A catalog record for this book is available from the British Library

ACKNOWLEDGMENTS
The publishers would like to thank the following artists who have contributed to this book:
Julian Baker, Mike Foster
All other artworks are from the Miles Kelly Artwork Bank

The publishers would like to thank the following sources for the use of their photographs:
Key: t = top, b = bottom, c = center, l = left, r = right,m = main, bg = background

Cover: (front) Steven Kazlowski/Naturepl.com; (back cl) Yobidaba/Shutterstock;
Page 6 Provided by the SeaWiFS Project, NASA/Goddard Space Flight Center, and ORBIMAGE; 9(br) micheldenijs/Shutterstock;
10(bg) tomos3/iStock; 11(cl) Bettmann/Getty, (bl) schaltwerk.de/Fotolia.com; 12 Tom Uhlman/Alamy; 13(cl) Getty Images AsiaPac/China
Photos/Getty; 14(b) ra-photos/iStock; 15(tr) anweber/Shutterstock, (br) AlbyDeTweede/iStock; 16(t) Nature Picture Library/Alamy,
(cr) joxxxxjo/iStock; 17(t) Dean Conger/Corbis Historical/Getty, (b) Getty Images AsiaPac/Ryan Pierse/Getty; 19(cl) www.firebox.com;
20 Arctic Images/Alamy Stock Photo; 21(tr) majorosl/iStock, (cr) Sunshine Solar Ltd, (bl) Gideon Mendel/Corbis Documentary/Getty;
22 Victor Habbick Visions/Science Photo Library; 23(br) AJSenviron/Alamy Stock Photo, (tl) Phil Schermeister/Corbis Historical/Getty;
24–25(bg) MARKA/Alamy Stock Photo, (tc) egdigital/iStock; 24(bl) Viviane Moos/Corbis Historical/Getty; 25(br) Sportstock/iStock;
26 David McNew/Getty Images North America/Getty; 27(tr) clintspencer/iStock, (cl) iStock, (b) John Dickson/Moment Open/Getty;
28(bg) David Kesti/Fotolia.com; 30(t) Design Pics Inc/Alamy Stock Photo, (b) AGRfoto/Alex Rowbotham/Alamy Stock Photo;
31(t) www.ecozone.co.uk, (b) Imagebroker/FLPA; 32(t) Kpzfoto/Alamy Stock Photo, (b) Christophe Simon/AFP/Getty; 33(tl) Martin
Harvey/Corbis Documentary/Getty; 34(t) Steve Estvanik/Fotolia.com, (b) Per-Anders Pettersson/Getty Images News/Getty;
35(t) Olga Alexandrova/Fotolia.com, (br) dejan750/iStock; 36(b) Lana/Fotolia.com; 37(t) Brian S.Turner/Corbis Documentary/Getty,
(br) iStock.com; 38(b) Katherine Feng/Globio/Minden Pictures/FLPA; 39(t) Jeremy Sutton-Hibbert/Alamy Stock Photo;
41(tl) Dimas Ardian/Stringer/Getty Images AsiaPac/Getty; 42(b) MiklG/Fotolia.com; 43 (main) David Wall/Alamy Stock Photo,
(t) Jeffrey L. Rotman/Corbis Documentary/Getty; 44 Igor Bakirov/Fotolia; 45(t) Imagegallery2/Alamy Stock Photo, (br) Bloomberg/Getty;
46–47 Mint Images/Frans Lanting/Getty

All other photographs are from: PhotoDisc

Every effort has been made to acknowledge the source and copyright holder of each picture.
Miles Kelly Publishing apologizes for any unintentional errors or omissions.

Made with paper from a sustainable forest

www.mileskelly.net

Contents

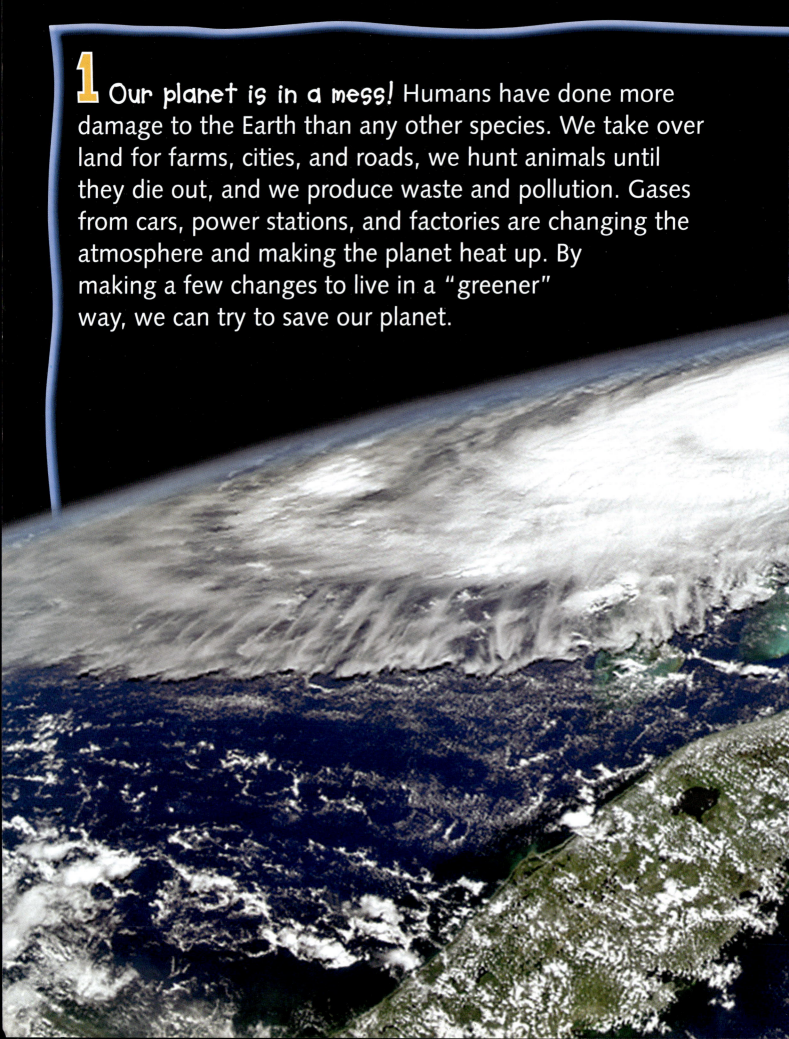

The Earth in danger

1 **Our planet is in a mess!** Humans have done more damage to the Earth than any other species. We take over land for farms, cities, and roads, we hunt animals until they die out, and we produce waste and pollution. Gases from cars, power stations, and factories are changing the atmosphere and making the planet heat up. By making a few changes to live in a "greener" way, we can try to save our planet.

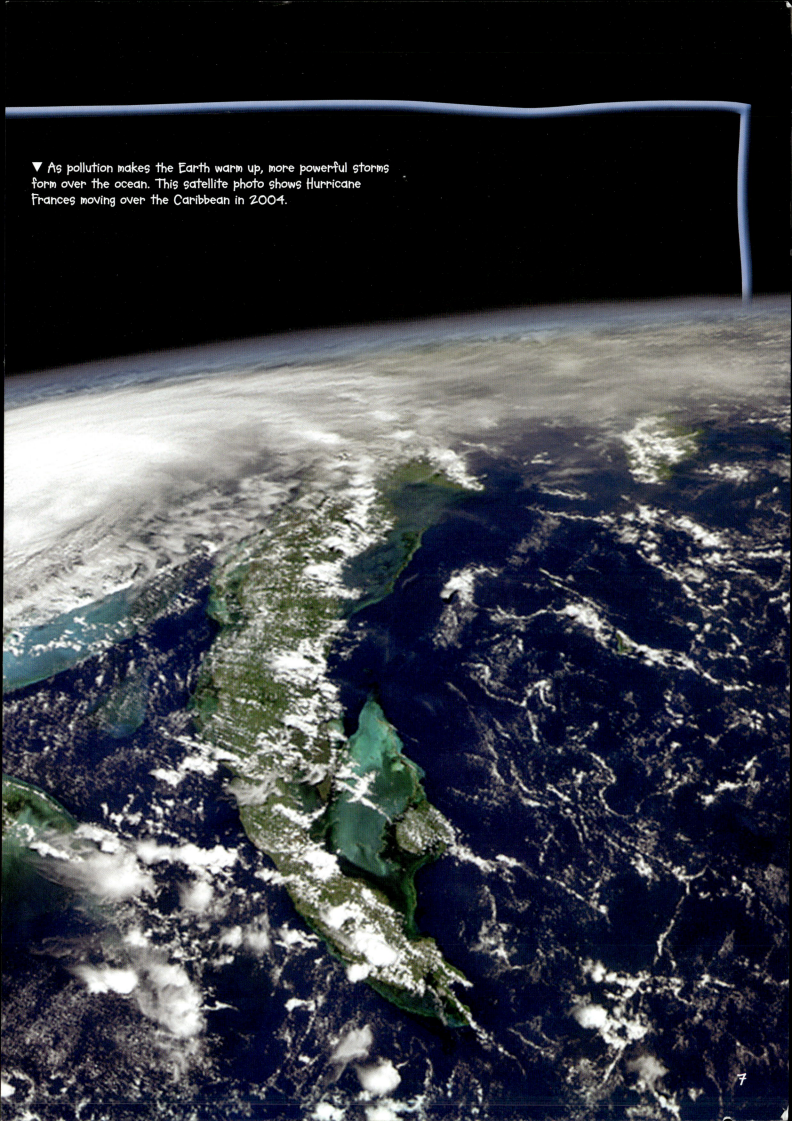

▼ As pollution makes the Earth warm up, more powerful storms form over the ocean. This satellite photo shows Hurricane Frances moving over the Caribbean in 2004.

7

Global warming

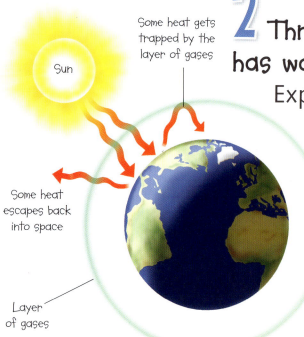

Sun

Some heat gets trapped by the layer of gases

Some heat escapes back into space

Layer of gases

▲ Global warming happens when greenhouse gases collect in the Earth's atmosphere. They let heat from the Sun through, but as it bounces back, it gets trapped close to the Earth, making the planet heat up.

2 Throughout its history, the Earth has warmed up and cooled down. Experts think that today's warming is down to humans—and it's happening faster than normal. Carbon dioxide and methane gases are released into the air as pollution. They are known as greenhouse gases and can stop the Sun's heat escaping from the atmosphere.

3 Global warming tells us that the climate is changing. Weather changes every day—we have hot days and cold days—but on average the climate is warming up. Scientists think that average temperatures have risen by 1.8 degrees Fahrenheit in the last 100 years, and that they will keep rising.

I DON'T BELIEVE IT!

Scientists think that sea levels could rise by more than 3 feet by 2100. Three million years ago when the Earth was hotter, the sea was 650 feet higher than today. We could be heading that way again.

4 Warmer temperatures mean wilder weather. Wind happens when air is heated and gets lighter. It rises up and cold air is sucked in to replace it. Rain occurs when heat makes water in rivers and oceans turn into vapor in the air. It rises up and forms rain clouds. Warmer temperatures mean more wind, rain, and storms.

KEY

◻ Average area of sea covered by ice from 1980–2000

◻ Predicted area of sea covered by ice for 2080–2100

ARCTIC OCEAN

◀ The ice in the Arctic Ocean is melting so fast that scientists think over half of it could be gone by 2100.

▼ Huge chunks of ice often break off into the sea at Paradise Bay, at the Antarctic.

5 **As the Earth heats up, its ice melts.** Vast areas of the Earth are covered in ice. It is found around the North and South Poles, and on high mountains. Now, because of global warming, more and more of this ice is melting. It turns into water and flows into the ocean. Also, as the water gets warmer, it expands (gets bigger) and the ocean takes up more space, making sea levels rise.

▶ Polar bears depend on large chunks of ice to hunt and rest on. Melting ice in the Arctic is making life much harder for them.

Energy crisis

6 We pump greenhouse gases into the atmosphere because we burn fuels to make energy. Cars, planes, and trains run on fuel, and we also burn it in power stations to produce electricity. The main fuels—coal, oil, and gas —are called fossil fuels because they formed underground over millions of years.

7 Fossil fuels are running out. Because they take so long to form, we are using up fossil fuels much faster than they can be replaced. Eventually, they will become so rare that it will be too expensive to find them. Experts think this will happen before the end of the 21st century.

▶ Oil and natural gas formed from the remains of tiny prehistoric ocean creatures that collected on the seabed. Layers of rock built up on top and squashed them. Over time, they became underground stores of oil, with pockets of gas above.

Oil platform drilling for oil and gas

Hard rock layer

Gas

Oil

Oil and gas move upward through soft rock layers until reaching a hard rock layer

The layer of dead ocean creatures is crushed by rock that forms above, and turns into oil and gas

Tiny ocean creatures die and sink to the seabed

QUIZ

Which of these things are used to supply electricity?
A. Burning coal B. Wind
C. The flow of rivers
D. Hamsters on wheels E. Sunshine
F. The energy of earthquakes

Answers:
A, B, C, and E. Hamsters could turn tiny turbines, but would make very little electricity. Earthquakes contain vast amounts of energy, but we have not found a way to harness it.

8 One thing we can do is find other fuels. Besides fossil fuels, we can burn fuels that come from plants. For example, the rape plant contains oil that can be burned in vehicle engines. However, burning these fuels still releases greenhouse gases.

9 Nuclear power is another kind of energy.

By splitting apart atoms—the tiny units that all materials are made of—energy is released, which can be turned into electricity. However, producing this energy creates toxic waste that can make people ill, and may be accidentally released into the air. Safer ways to use nuclear power are being researched.

▲ The Grand Coulee Dam in Washington, holds back a river, creating a lake, or reservoir. Water is let through the dam to turn turbines, which create electricity.

10 Lots of energy is produced without burning anything.

Hydroelectric power stations use the pushing power of flowing rivers to turn turbines. Hydroelectricity is a renewable, or green, energy source—it doesn't use anything up or cause pollution. Scientists are also working on ways to turn the movement of waves and tides into usable energy.

11 The wind and the Sun are great renewable sources of energy, too.

Wind turbines turn generators, which convert the "turning movement" into electricity. Solar panels work by collecting sunlight and turning it into an electrical current.

◀ Solar panels are made of materials that soak up sunlight and turn its energy into a flow of electricity.

Rotor blade

▲ Modern wind turbines usually have three blades, which spin around at speed in high winds.

On the move

12 **Cars release a lot of greenhouse gases.** No one had a car 200 years ago. Now, there are around 500 million cars in the world and most are used daily. Cars burn gasoline or diesel fuel, which are made from oil—a fossil fuel. We can reduce greenhouse gases and slow down global warming by using cars less.

Carbon dioxide (CO_2)

Nitrogen dioxide (NO_2)

Sulfur dioxide (SO_2)

▲ Car exhaust fumes contain harmful, polluting gases, including sulfur dioxide, nitrogen dioxide, and carbon dioxide, which are poisonous to humans.

13 **Public transportation is made up of buses, trams, and trains that everyone can use.** Buses can carry 60 or 70 people at once and trains can carry several hundred. They still burn fuel, but they release much less greenhouse gases per person than cars.

▼ In many cities, there are so many cars that they cause big traffic jams. They move slowly with their engines running, churning out even more pollution.

COUNT YOUR STEPS

Besides saving on greenhouse gases, walking is great exercise and helps you stay healthy. Try counting your steps for one whole day. How many can you do—3,000, 5,000, or even 10,000?

14 Planes fly long distances at high speeds, giving out tons of greenhouse gases on each journey. A return flight from the UK to the USA releases more carbon dioxide than a car does in one year. Where you can, travel by boat or train for shorter jouneys.

▲ Maglev trains use magnets to hover above the rails. The magnetic force propels the train forward, rather than a gasoline or diesel-burning engine.

▲ Cyclists in Beijing, China, enjoy World Car Free Day. This was organized to help reduce pollution.

◀ This graph shows the world's top ten producers of carbon dioxide pollution (carbon dioxide is a major greenhouse gas). These figures are based on emissions in 2015.

CO₂ emissions (millions of tons)

11,000
10,000
9,000
8,000
7,000
6,000
5,000
4,000
3,000
2,000
1,000
0

China
USA
India
Russia
Japan
Germany
Iran
South Korea
Canada
Saudi Arabia

15 The greenest way to get around is to walk. For short journeys, walk instead of going by car. Inside buildings, use the stairs instead of taking elevators. Cycling is good, too. A bicycle doesn't burn any fuels, it just uses the power of your legs.

16 Long ago, before engines and turbines were invented, transportation worked differently. Boats had sails or oars and were driven by wind or human power, and carts and carriages were pulled by animals. As fossil fuels run out, we may see some old means of transportation coming back.

Save energy at home

17 Saving electricity at home reduces pollution. Most electricity we use is produced from burning fossil fuels. By using less of it, we can cut greenhouse gas emissions. Always turn off lights, TVs, computers, and other electrical devices when not in use. Low energy light bulbs are a good idea, too. They use less power and last longer.

FIVE ENERGY-SAVING TIPS

Turn appliances off properly
Switch appliances off at the "off" switch or at the plug. Appliances left in standby mode still use electricity.

Make sure your cooking pots have lids on
This saves energy by reducing cooking time.

Don't overfill your kettle
Just boil the amount of water that you need—this will save energy.

Buy fresh foods instead of frozen
Much more energy is used to produce frozen foods, so buy fresh when you can.

Turn down your heating by one degree
You won't really notice the difference, and you could save around 10 percent off your energy bill.

▼ Washing hung outside dries in the heat of the Sun. This saves on electricity and fossil fuels.

18 Your washing can be green as well as clean! Tumble dryers dry quickly, but they use lots of electricity. In summer, peg your clothes out on a washing line in the garden. In winter, hang them on a drier close to a radiator. You can save even more energy by washing clothes at a lower temperature.

19 We invent all kinds of electrical gadgets to do things for us, but do we really need them? You can save energy by sweeping the floor instead of using a vacuum cleaner every time. Use your hands to make bread, instead of a food processor. Avoid electrical can openers, knives, and other power hungry gadgets.

I DON'T BELIEVE IT!

Only 10 percent of the electricity used by an old-style light bulb is turned into light. The rest turns into wasted heat, which also makes it burn out quicker.

20

Solar panels are a green way to power a home. They work the same way that solar powered calculators do—they can change sunlight into electricity straight away. If a home produces more electricity than it needs, it can sell some back to the local energy provider.

▼ Solar panels are often made of silicon. When sunlight hits the silicon, electrical charges can flow as an electrical current.

▲ Solar panels can be installed on rooftops to provide power for homes.

Sunlight

Sunlight

Wires carry the flow of electricity to appliances, such as lights

Solar panel

▼ Growing turf on the roof is a good way to insulate a house to prevent heat from escaping and being wasted. The grass uses up CO_2, and makes oxygen, too.

21

Turn down the heating in your house and keep warm in other ways! If you're cold put on an extra sweater, or wrap up warm under a cozy blanket or duvet. You will also save energy if your home has insulation in the walls and roof, and double-glazed windows.

Green shopping

22 Most people buy something from a shop every day. Items such as food, clothes, and furniture take a lot of energy to grow, manufacture, and then transport to the shops. By doing some smart shopping, you can save some of that energy.

▲ Old plastic bags fill up landfill sites and take hundreds of years to rot away. They can also harm wildlife and farm animals.

▶ Bags made from cloth can be used over and over again.

QUIZ

1. Which kind of shopping bag is greenest—plastic, paper, or cloth?

2. Which is more expensive—a shop-bought bottle of water or the same amount of tap water?

3. What is vintage clothing?

Answers:
1. A reusable cloth bag
2. Bottled water costs up to 1,000 times more than tap water
3. Secondhand clothes

23 Say no to plastic bags! Plastic bags are made from oil—a fossil fuel—and it takes energy to make them. However, we often use them once then throw them away, which creates litter and pollution. When you go shopping take a reusable bag made from cloth, or reuse old plastic bags so that you don't have to use new ones.

24 How far has your food traveled? The distance food has been transported is called "food miles." You can reduce food miles by shopping at farm shops and local markets. Check food packages to find food that was produced nearby. Food that has traveled a long way is greener if it came by boat, and not by plane.

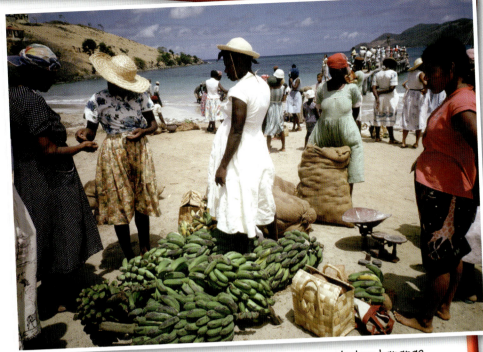

▲ On the island of Saint Vincent in the Caribbean, people buy bananas that have been grown locally. Bananas grown here are also shipped to other countries—a much greener way to transport them than by plane.

25 More and more people are buying bottled water. Water is heavy and a lot of fuel is needed to transport it long distances. The plastic bottles create waste and cause pollution, too. It's greener to use clean, pure water from the faucet at home.

▼ This paper shows that anything can be recycled! Roo Poo paper is made from 80 percent recycled paper and 20 percent kangaroo droppings.

GENUINE ROO POO PAPER

26 Buying secondhand goods is a great way to save energy. When you buy secondhand clothes, furniture, or books nothing new has to be made in a factory. Antique furniture and vintage clothes are often better quality than new things—and more individual, too.

Reduce, reuse, recycle

27 **Most of us buy more than we need.** We want the latest clothes, toys, and cars even though we may not need them—this is called consumerism. Reduce, reuse, and recycle is a good way to remember what we can do to reduce the amount of things we buy.

28 **To start with, reduce your shopping.** Do you or your family ever buy things that don't end up getting used? Next time, think before you buy—be sure that you are going to use it. Buying less means fewer things have to be made, transported, and thrown away. It saves money, too!

Empty glass bottles go into a recycling bin

▶ Recycling materials greatly reduces the amount of energy needed to make new products. This graph shows how much energy is saved in making new products using recycled materials, rather than raw materials.

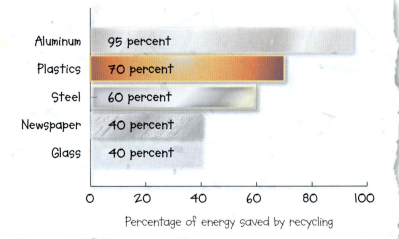

Aluminum	95 percent
Plastics	70 percent
Steel	60 percent
Newspaper	40 percent
Glass	40 percent

0   20   40   60   80   100

Percentage of energy saved by recycling

29 **Recycling means that materials can be made into new things instead of thrown away.** This saves energy and makes less waste. Paper, cardboard, food cans, glass, and some plastics can all be recycled. Some local authorities collect them, or you can take them to a recycling collection point at a school, supermarket, or dump.

The bottles are collected from the bin and transported to a glass recycling plant

The old, broken glass is cleaned and melted down with other substances

30 We live in a "throwaway society." We are used to disposable things that get used once, then go in the trash. When something breaks, it's easy to get another, but making and transporting these new things uses up raw materials, and creates pollution. Reuse some of the things you throw away—mend clothes by sewing on a new button, pocket, or patch and use empty food containers to store things in.

I DON'T BELIEVE IT!

Many things we buy are built to break easily. This is called "built-in obsolescence." Manufacturers hope that when your things break, you'll buy new ones—from them.

▼ These shopping bags have been made from old, recycled food sacks. They save on raw materials and cut down on plastic bags.

31 If you can't reuse something yourself, maybe someone else can. Give old clothes, furniture, books, and toys to a Goodwill store, or sell them at a yard sale.

The bottles are sold and used, and can then be recycled again

▼ Recycled glass is used in road surfaces, concrete production, and a finely ground glass is used to fill golf bunkers. New bottles and jars are also made from recycled glass.

The bottles are filled with drinks and labeled

The liquid glass is blow molded (blown with air) into new bottles

Green machines

32 As well as using machines less, we can use greener ones. Cars, computers, and electrical appliances don't have to use lots of energy. Scientists are working on greener versions that use less electricity or fuel—or even none at all.

33 When hydrogen gas burns, it doesn't release any greenhouse gases— just water. Today, some cars run on hydrogen and create no pollution. However, making the hydrogen for them to run on uses up electricity, and in turn fossil fuels. As fossil fuels run out and renewable energy sources take over, hydrogen cars may become common.

I DON'T BELIEVE IT!

The fastest human-powered vehicles are recumbent cycles, which the rider drives in a lying-down position. They can travel at over 80 miles per hour.

▼ A hydrogen-powered car and a hydrogen fuel station show what more of us could be using in the future.

Hydrogen
Fuel station Vetnisstöð

HYDROGEN3 GM
GM FUEL CELL TECHNOLOGY

HYDROGEN3

34 You might have traveled on an electric train or bus before. Instead of burning fuel, they run on electricity supplied from a large, onboard battery or overhead cables. This means less air pollution in city centers.

▲ Trams like this can be found in many cities around the world. They work by collecting electricity from overhead wires or cables.

35 Did you know that "white goods" can be green? White goods are refrigerators, washing machines, dishwashers, and other kitchen appliances. New ones have a rating showing how green they are. The greenest ones use the least energy and supplies such as water. Now you can choose the best ones for the planet.

▶ This solar powered phone charger uses solar panels to turn sunlight into an electricity supply.

◀ As well as saving on electricity, windup radios are very useful in parts of the world where there is no electricity supply, such as parts of Africa.

36 Windup power was once used for toys, but now there are windup radios, flashlights, and phone chargers. The handle is wound and the energy from this movement is turned into an electricity supply inside the machine. Windup machines save on fossil fuels and reduce greenhouse gases.

Science solutions

▼ An artist's impression of a space shield that could be used to shade the Earth from the Sun.

37 Using less energy is one way to slow down global warming, but there might be others, too. Scientists are coming up with all kinds of space-age and hi-tech solutions that could help the Earth to cool down again.

38 Maybe we could shade the Earth to cool it down. Scientists have lots of ideas about how to do this. Some of these include launching huge mirrors into space to reflect the Sun's light and heat away, or filling the atmosphere with tiny particles to blot out the Sun. Another is to spread out a fine mesh, like a giant sheet, into space to make a sunshade. So far, all of these ideas are far too expensive to try.

I DON'T BELIEVE IT!

In a single day a cow can give out 18 cubic feet of methane gas. That's enough to fill more than 100 party balloons!

39

Instead of greenhouse gases filling the air, we could soak them up. Plants naturally take in carbon dioxide (CO_2)—a greenhouse gas—so planting lots of trees helps to slow global warming. Scientists are also trying to develop special types of algae (tiny plants) that can soak up even more greenhouse gases.

▶ A huge cloud of green algae can be seen near the shore of Lake Tahoe. Algae is made up of millions of tiny plants. There is so much algae in the world that it soaks up a lot of the world's carbon dioxide.

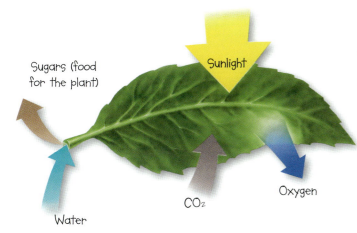

Sugars (food for the plant)

Sunlight

Oxygen

CO_2

Water

▲ Plants make food using sunlight, by a process called photosynthesis. They use up carbon dioxide and give out oxygen.

40

We could catch greenhouse gases before they escape into the air. There are already devices that can do this, which capture carbon dioxide from power stations and factory chimneys. Once it is caught, the gas needs to be stored safely. Scientists are looking at ways of storing carbon dioxide, or changing it into something harmless.

▼ A special foam wrapping is unrolled over the Tortin glacier in Switzerland to stop it melting.

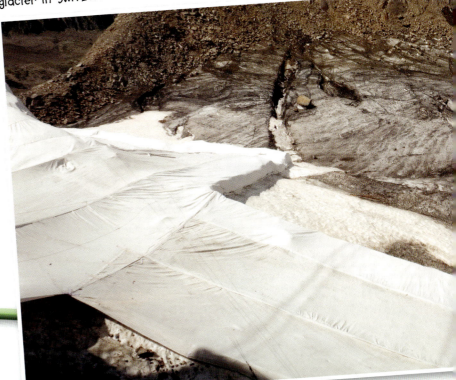

41

As they digest grass, cows and other grazing animals pass a lot of wind! This gas contains methane—a greenhouse gas. Besides burning fuels, this is one of the biggest causes of global warming. Scientists are experimenting with feeding cows different foods to reduce the amount of methane.

Pollution problems

42 **Pollution means dirt, waste, and other substances that damage our surroundings.** Our farms and factories often release harmful chemicals into rivers and lakes, and cars, lorries, and other road vehicles give out poisonous, polluting gases. Litter and trash are pollution, too.

▼ A thick layer of smog hangs over the city of Bangkok, the capital of Thailand.

43 **Humans make waste when we go to the bathroom.** The waste and water from our toilets is called sewage. This usually ends up at sewage works where we process it to make it safe, but in some places sewage flows straight into rivers or the sea. It is smelly and dirty and can contain deadly germs.

44 **Pollution can harm our health.** Smog is a mixture of smoke from factories and motor vehicles, and fog, and it collects over some cities. It makes it harder to breathe, worsening illnesses such as asthma.

◄ People in Kuala Lumpur, the capital of Malaysia, wear masks to avoid breathing in smog.

◀ People who live near airports have to put up with the sound of low flying planes over their houses.

45

Even noise is a kind of pollution. Airport noise disturbs the people who live nearby, and loud noises from ships and submarines can disturb whales. These intelligent animals rely on their own sounds to navigate and communicate, so other noises can confuse them.

46

The more we throw away, the more trash piles up. When we drop trash just anywhere, it becomes litter. If we dispose of it properly, some of it may get recycled, and the rest gets taken away and dumped in a big hole in the ground, called a landfill site. Either way, there's too much of it!

47

Air pollution can cause acid rain. The waste gases from power stations and factories mix with water droplets in clouds and form weak acid. This makes soil, rivers, and lakes more acidic, which can kill fish and plants. Acid rain can even make rock dissolve.

▶ At landfill sites, trash piles up, making huge mountains of waste that have to be flattened down by rollers.

TRUE OR FALSE?

1. Trash isn't a problem if you put it in a trash can.
2. Acid rain can make your nose fall off.
3. Loud noises in the ocean can make whales get lost.

Answers:
1. FALSE—it still piles up in landfill sites 2. FALSE— the acid isn't strong enough. But it can dissolve away the stone nose of a statue 3. TRUE—according to some scientists

Litter and trash

48 **After leaving your house, trash has a long life ahead of it.** Things such as banana skins will rot away quickly, but man-made products such as plastics take a long time to decay and break down. That's why landfill sites fill up fast, and we have to find more and more space for our trash.

◄ Forest fires caused by dropped litter, such as glass bottles and cigarette ends, can be deadly and cost a lot of money to put out. Here, a helicopter drops water onto a forest fire.

49 **A drinks bottle left in a dry field or forest could start a fire.** The curved glass in a bottle—especially a piece of a broken bottle—can act like a magnifying glass. If it focuses the Sun's heat on a dry patch of grass, a fire can start.

I DON'T BELIEVE IT!

People drop the most litter from cars because they think they can make a quick getaway! However, governments are making new laws to stop littering from cars.

► This is litter on a much bigger scale—dumping large trash items instead of disposing of them legally and safely.

50 Some people treat the countryside and other public places as a dumping ground. Big items, such as mattresses, sofas, and shopping carts, are sometimes dumped on roadsides or in rivers. Besides looking a mess, these things can release poisons as they rot away.

▲ Ducks struggle through a pond polluted with plastic bottles.

51 The plastic rings that hold cans together can be deadly for wildlife. These stretchy loops are used to hold drinks cans together in packs. As litter, they can get caught around the neck of a wild animal, such as a seagull, and strangle it. Snip the loops open with scissors before throwing them in the bin.

▼ Fishing nets left on beaches can endanger wildlife. This one has become tangled around a sea lion's neck.

52 Fishing weights and lines left near rivers and lakes can choke or strangle water wildlife. Weights sometimes contain lead and this can poison water birds, such as swans. People who go fishing should make sure they never leave any of their equipment behind.

Reducing waste

53 There are lots of things you can do to reduce waste. When you throw something away, think if it could be recycled or reused instead. Avoid buying things that will have to be thrown away after one use.

MAKE SOME COMPOST

Make a heap of plant waste, fruit and vegetable skins, and grass cuttings in a corner of your garden. It takes a few months to turn into compost. To help it along, mix it around and dig it over with a garden fork. When the compost is ready, you can use it for potting plants or add it to soil in your garden.

▲ You can buy a specially made compost bin to make compost in, like this one.

54 Instead of throwing away fruit and vegetable peelings, turn them into compost. When your peelings rot down, they turn into a rich, fertile soil that's great for your garden. All you need is a space outside where you can pile up your waste for composting, or you can get a special compost bin.

The composting process

1. Waste, including fruit and vegetable peelings, leaves, and eggshells, goes in the top.

2. Tiny organisms called microbes start to break down the waste, which makes it heat up.

3. Insects help to break it down even more and worms help air to get into the compost.

4. The compost is brown and moist and should smell earthy.

55 Millions of disposable batteries end up in landfill sites every year. They take a long time to decay and when they do, they release harmful chemicals. Rechargeable batteries can be refilled with energy from the mains and reused many times.

56 Reduce your waste by picking reusables, not disposables. Face wipes and disposable diapers, cups, and cooking trays are all things that we use once, then throw away. It's greener to use reuseables, such as washable baking trays, cloth tea towels, and washable diapers.

57 Lots of the things we buy come wrapped up several times over. We take them home, unwrap them, and throw the packaging away. Choose products with less packaging, or none at all.

▼ Much of our trash is made up of pointless packaging that we don't really need.

TIME TO DECOMPOSE

Fruit and vegetables	2 days to 6 months
Newspaper	6 months
Drinks cans	100 to 500 years
Disposable diapers	200 to 500 years
Plastic bags	450 years
Plastic bottles	100 to 1,000 years +

Cutting pollution

58 Big companies need to cut the pollution they produce. There are laws to ban them dumping toxic chemicals and to limit dangerous waste gases, but they're not yet tough enough to make a big difference. Pressure groups such as Greenpeace are fighting for stronger, better laws.

▲ This tractor is spraying chemicals onto crops to kill pests and weeds. When it rains the chemicals wash into rivers and can harm wildlife.

59 Weedkillers and insect sprays kill unwanted plants and bugs in the garden. However, because they are poisonous they can kill other wildlife too, and cause pollution. It's greener to pull up weeds and pick off pests instead.

▼ This tractor is using a different method—cutting back weeds between the crops, instead of spraying them. This keeps the environment cleaner.

60
Cleaning your house can make the planet dirty! Strong cleaning chemicals that are washed down the sink can end up in water supplies. Try to use less of them, or use natural, homemade alternatives. A mixture of water and vinegar is great for cleaning windows.

▶ Some companies are now making reuseable washing balls that clean clothes without using any detergent.

61
Paint, paint stripper, and varnish contain toxic chemicals. These chemicals don't break down naturally when they are poured away, which results in pollution. If you can, save them to use again, or see if your local authorities will collect them for reusing.

62
Shampoo, face creams, and makeup are full of polluting chemicals. Pick greener products that contain natural ingredients. You can even use everyday ingredients, such as olive oil, to make your own skin treatments.

▲ Soap nuts are berries of the soapberry tree. They contain a natural, soapy chemical that can be used to wash clothes.

MAKE A FOOT SOAK

Mix together:
1 tablespoon of fine oatmeal
1 tablespoon of skimmed milk powder
1 teaspoonful of dried rosemary

Spoon the mixture into an old, clean sock and tie a knot at the top. Leave the sock in a bowl of warm water for a few minutes, then soak your feet in the water for 20 minutes.

Wildlife in danger

▲ Wild animals, such as crocodiles, are still killed for their skins to make items such as handbags and rugs.

63 Since humans have existed on Earth, many living things have been destroyed. To make space for cities, farms, and roads, people have taken over wild areas, and plants and animals have lost their natural homes, or habitats. This is called habitat loss and it is the main reason why wildlife is in danger.

▼ This bird is covered in oil spilled from an oil tanker (a ship that carries oil). If birds like this aren't cleaned, they will die.

64 Toxic waste, oil spills, and pesticides can be deadly for wildlife. In the 1950s, a chemical called DDT was used to kill insects on crops, but it affected other animals including wild birds. It made them lay eggs with very thin shells that cracked easily. The birds began to die out as they could not have chicks.

65 Wild plants and animals suffer when we exploit them (use them to meet our needs). Humans hunt wild animals for their skins, meat, and other body parts, such as ivory from elephants' tusks. Some people steal wild plants, too. If too many are taken, their numbers fall fast.

◄ These nature reserve wardens in Dzanga–Ndoki National Park in the Central African Republic have caught some poachers hunting protected animals.

QUIZ

What do these words mean?
1. Extinct 2. Species
3. Endangered 4. Habitat

Answers:
1. Died out and no longer existing. 2. A particular type of living thing. 3. In danger of becoming extinct. 4. The surroundings where a plant or animal lives

66 Human activities have wiped out some species, or types, of living things. When a species no longer exists, it is said to be extinct. The great auk—a large-beaked, black-and-white sea bird—became extinct in the 1850s due to hunting by humans. Many other species are now close to extinction, including the tiger and mountain gorilla.

▼ The orangutan (a type of ape) is an extremely threatened species, and one of our closest animal cousins.

67 When a creature is in danger of becoming extinct, we call it threatened. Severely threatened species are known as endangered. These labels help to teach people about the dangers to wildlife. They also help us to make laws to try to protect these species from hunters and collectors.

Saving habitats

68 To save wildlife, we need to save habitats. Humans are taking up more and more space and if we don't slow down, there'll be no wild, natural land left. We need to leave plenty of natural areas for wildlife to live in.

▲ These penguins live in Antarctica. Their habitat is ice and freezing water and it could be affected by global warming.

69 One hundred years ago, people went on safari to hunt animals. Today, more tourists go to watch wild animals and plants in their natural habitat—this is called ecotourism and it helps wildlife. Local people can make enough money from tourism, so they don't need to hunt. However, ecotourism can disturb wildlife, so tourists have to take care where they go.

► Tourists in a jeep approach a pride of lions in a nature reserve in South Africa.

70 Nature reserves and national parks are safe homes for wildlife. The land is kept wild and unspoiled to preserve natural habitats. There are also guards or wardens to protect the wildlife and watch out for hunters.

▲ As the human population continues to rise, more and more wild, natural land is being taken over.

71 It can be hard for humans to preserve habitats because we need space too. There are more than 7 billion (7,000,000,000) humans on Earth today. Experts think this will rise to at least 9 billion. Some countries have laws to limit the number of children people are allowed to have to try to control the population.

▼ A diver explores a coral reef. The corals are home to many species of fish, crabs, and shellfish.

72 You can help to keep habitats safe. Don't take stones, flowers, or shells from the countryside. Visit nature reserves—your money helps to run them. Don't buy souvenirs made of coral, or other animals or plants, as this encourages hunting and habitat destruction.

I DON'T BELIEVE IT!

The river Thames in London, England, has just 10 percent of the pollution it had in the 1950s because of preventative actions. It is now home to over 100 species of fish.

In the garden

73 If you have a garden at home or at school, you could make it into a safe place for wildlife to live. Gardens are parts of towns and cities that can stay wild. They can be a good habitat for many species of small animals and wild plants.

◀ An insect box provides a home for creatures, such as bees and ladybugs.

74 Wild creatures love a messy garden. If gardens are always tidy there is nowhere for animals to hide. Leave parts of your garden untidy and overgrown—let grass and weeds grow and don't clear up piles of leaves. These areas provide shelter and homes for spiders, beetles, and birds.

▼ Gardeners in Europe may be lucky enough to see hedgehogs. These prickly little animals eat many common garden pests.

FOOD FOR BIRDS

Here are some snacks to try putting out for garden birds:
Grated hard cheese
Raisins
Sunflower seeds or other seeds
Chopped or crushed nuts
Meat scraps
Fresh, chopped coconut

Avoid putting out dry or salty food, such as stale bread or salted nuts, as it's bad for birds.

75 **You can help wild birds by feeding them.** Feed birds in winter—there are fewer berries and insects for them to eat at this time of year. Put up a bird table, or hang bird feeders from trees in your garden.

▲ Butterflies such as tortoiseshells like to feed on the flowers of a buddleia bush.

◄ A coal tit and a red squirrel are helping themselves to nuts from this bird feeder.

76 **Bees and butterflies feed on nectar—a sweet juice found inside flowers.** A garden full of flowers will provide lots of food for insects. They especially like sunflowers, lavender, and buddleia bushes.

► Sunflowers are great for wildlife. They provide nectar for insects and nutritious seeds for birds.

77 **Thick, thorny bushes are brilliant for birds.** Some bushes, such as brambles and hawthorns, provide berries that birds like to eat. Thick, tangled bushes also make safe places for birds to build their nests or hide from animals, such as pet cats.

Saving species

78 Goods made from threatened wildlife species can be bought around the world. Although there are laws to protect plants and animals, they are often broken. It's best not to buy anything that might come from a threatened species, such as ivory, skins, horns, or bones.

◀ Parrots are sometimes stolen from the wild as chicks and sold as pets.

80 You or your class could sponsor an endangered animal, such as a tiger. You pay a small fee that goes towards caring for the animal and running the reserve where it lives. In return, you'll get letters or emails about your animal's progress. Wildlife organizations can help you to do this.

79 Exotic pets can be exciting, but they are sometimes stolen from the wild. Avoid having an unusual pet such as a rare lizard or parrot. It could be a threatened species that has been taken away from its natural habitat.

◄ A Greenpeace ship encounters a whaling ship, the Nisshin Maru, in the Antarctic Ocean. Some countries still hunt whales, but campaigning groups such as Greenpeace are trying to stop it.

I DON'T BELIEVE IT!

Millions of sharks, including threatened species, are hunted every year to make shark's fin soup. The soup is an expensive delicacy in China.

81 **People still hunt threatened species, even though it's illegal.** Many people in the world are very poor and some can't resist hunting a threatened tiger to sell its skin, or a shark to sell its fins. Governments need to try to reduce poverty, to help wildlife as well as people.

82 **To help endangered animals, visit your nearest zoo.** Most zoos have captive breeding programs. These help endangered animals to have babies to increase their numbers. Some can then be released back into the wild.

▼ In China, giant pandas are being bred successfully on wildlife reserves. These are just some of the new babies born in recent years.

Forests and farms

83 More than 46,000 square miles of forests are logged (cut down) every year. That's an area the size of the country of Malawi in Africa, or the state of Pennsylvania. Trees do grow again, but we are cutting forests down much faster than they can grow back.

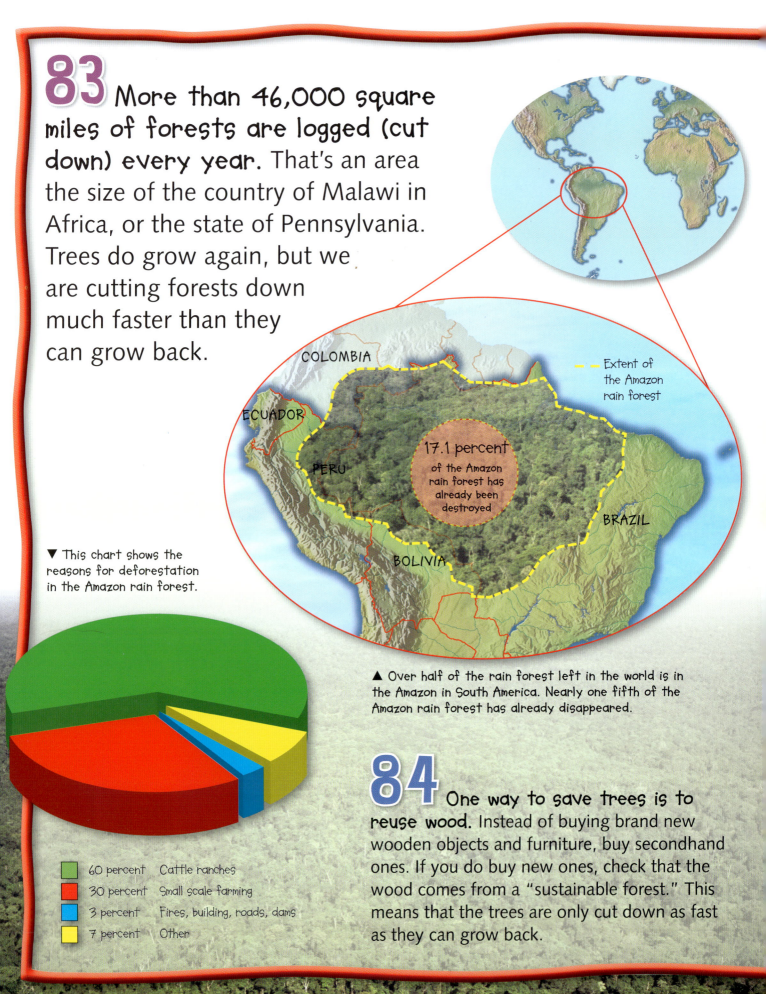

▼ This chart shows the reasons for deforestation in the Amazon rain forest.

COLOMBIA

ECUADOR

PERU

- - - Extent of the Amazon rain forest

17.1 percent
of the Amazon rain forest has already been destroyed

BOLIVIA

BRAZIL

▲ Over half of the rain forest left in the world is in the Amazon in South America. Nearly one fifth of the Amazon rain forest has already disappeared.

🟩	60 percent	Cattle ranches
🟥	30 percent	Small scale farming
🟦	3 percent	Fires, building, roads, dams
🟨	7 percent	Other

84 One way to save trees is to reuse wood. Instead of buying brand new wooden objects and furniture, buy secondhand ones. If you do buy new ones, check that the wood comes from a "sustainable forest." This means that the trees are only cut down as fast as they can grow back.

▲ Large areas of rain forest in Indonesia and Malaysia have been cut down to make way for oil palm tree plantations. The fruits of the oil palm are harvested for their oil, which can be found in one in ten supermarket products.

85 Farms take up almost 40 percent of the Earth's land. We need farms to provide us with food—to grow crops and keep animals on—but they have a big impact on the Earth. Most farmland is devoted to one type of crop or animal, so many types of wildlife that live there lose their homes.

86 Organic farming can be a greener way to farm. It doesn't use artificial chemicals, such as pesticides and fertilizers, which means it is good for wildlife and the soil. If you buy organic food and other products, you help to keep the Earth cleaner.

I DON'T BELIEVE IT!

In prehistoric times, forests covered more than half of the Earth's land. Today, almost half of those forests have gone.

▶ As most nuts grow on trees, they are one crop that can be grown without cutting them down.

87 Buying nuts can help save the rain forests. Some products, such as brazil nuts, grow on rain forest trees. By buying them, you are helping farmers to keep rain forests alive, instead of cutting them down to grow other crops.

Seas and coasts

88 Seas and oceans cover the biggest part of the Earth's surface—nearly three quarters of it! Pollution, global warming, and fishing have a huge effect on the sea and its wildlife.

I DON'T BELIEVE IT!

Some cities, towns, and farms are actually below sea level! A quarter of the Netherlands is lower than the ocean. The water is held back by barriers such as dams, dikes, and levees.

89 Pollution from farms, factories, and houses often flows into rivers and ends up in the ocean. Tiny ocean plants and animals absorb the chemicals. When they are eaten by larger ocean creatures, the polluting chemicals are passed on from one animal to the next. Many large creatures, such as sharks and polar bears, have been found to have a lot of toxic chemicals in their bodies.

90 Coastal areas are in trouble because of rising sea levels. As the ocean rises, tides, tsunamis, and storm waves can reach further inland. If the ocean rises much more, it could put many coastal cities underwater. The danger of the ocean flooding the land is one of the biggest reasons to try to slow global warming down.

◀ In Thailand, signs on beaches and streets give warnings and provide evacuation directions to be used in the event of a tsunami. Thailand is one of the countries that was devastated by the tsunami that struck on December 26, 2004.

91 For thousands of years, humans have hunted fish. Today, we are catching so many fish that some types are in danger of disappearing—this is called overfishing. To try to stop it, there are laws to give fishing boats a quota, or limit, on how many fish they can catch.

▼ Low-lying islands, such as this one in Fiji, are in danger of disappearing as sea levels rise.

▶ Cod is one type of fish that has been overfished in some parts of the world.

92 There's precious treasure in the sea bed. It contains oil—a fossil fuel—and many other useful minerals. However, drilling and digging into the sea bed damages wildlife and sea habitats, such as coral reefs. Governments are starting to set up nature reserves in the sea, as well as on land. In these areas, no mining or drilling is allowed.

◀ Oil rigs such as this one are built around a giant drill that bores into the sea bed to extract oil.

Water resources

93 The world is using too much water.
In many places, water is being pumped out of lakes, rivers, and underground wells faster than rain can replace it. As the human population grows, so will the need for water.

▼ Most of the world's freshwater is frozen! The figures below show where the fresh water is found.

Ice caps and glaciers
77.2 percent

Ground water
22.26 percent

Rivers and lakes
0.32 percent

Soil
0.18 percent

Atmosphere
0.04 percent

94 Global warming is causing huge water problems.
Some areas are getting more rain and floods, as hotter temperatures lead to more clouds and storms. Floods often pollute water supplies. Other places are becoming hotter and drier, leading to droughts. Either way, global warming is leading to water shortages.

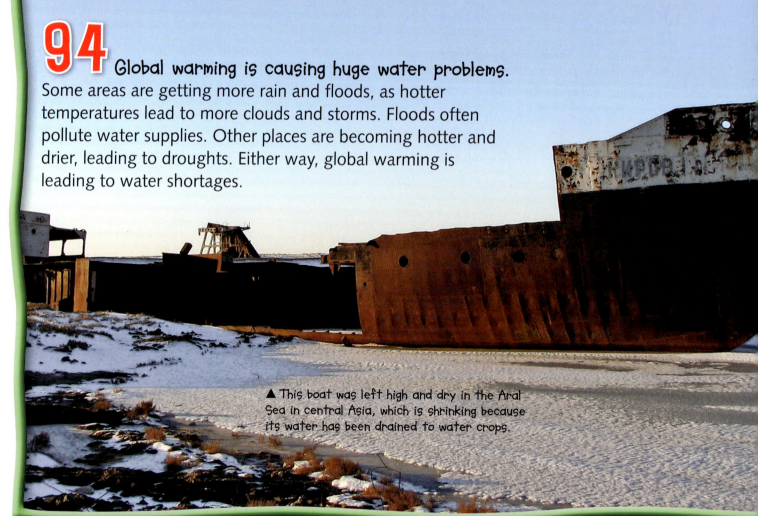
▲ This boat was left high and dry in the Aral Sea in central Asia, which is shrinking because its water has been drained to water crops.

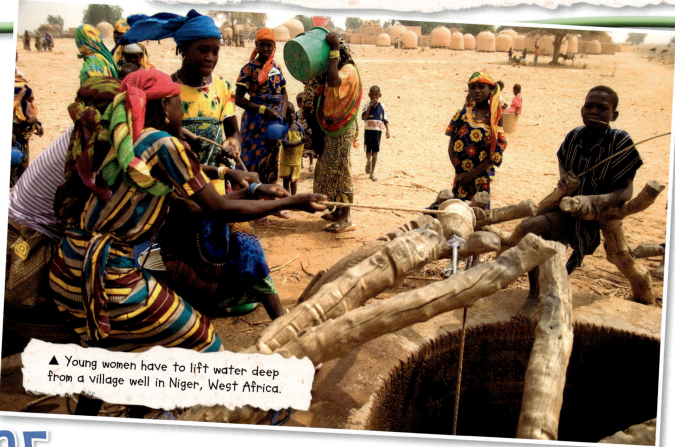

▲ Young women have to lift water deep from a village well in Niger, West Africa.

95

In some countries, drinking water comes from the sea. Seawater is much too salty to drink, but in dry countries, such as Kuwait, they have factories called desalination plants. They take the salt out of seawater to make it fit to drink. However, this process uses up lots of energy and is not a long-term solution.

96

Having a green garden saves water! Many people pave their gardens over for a patio, but rain flows straight off the hard surface and can lead to floods. If gardens are kept as soil and plants, rain soaks into the ground and keeps water supplies topped up.

▼ An aerial view of a desalination plant in Kuwait.

Seawater enters here and is forced through the filter

Salt molecules cannot pass through the filter

Fine filter

Water molecule

▲ The salt is removed from seawater by pushing it through a very fine filter, making it drinkable. This process is called reverse osmosis.

The environment around us

97 **The word environment means the place that surrounds us.** Planet Earth and all the habitats on it make up our environment. That's why being green is sometimes called environmentalism.

▶ We need to let as much of the Earth as possible stay in its natural state, such as this beautiful forest in Borneo.

98 **As this book shows, the Earth is changing too fast.** To be green, and to care for the environment, we need to change the Earth as little as possible. We must reduce the litter, pollution, and greenhouse gases that we produce. At the same time we must take less away from it.

TURN YOUR SCHOOL GREEN

One thing you can do to help save the Earth is persuade your school to go green (or greener).

Here are some ideas:

- Arrange a recycling rota to collect waste paper from all the classrooms and offices.
- Make posters to put up in the toilets to remind people to save water.
- If there's space, set up a school wildlife garden and compost heap—persuade the kitchen staff to compost food leftovers.

99 Being green is a job for everyone. At home, switching off lights and saving water helps to save the Earth. Towns, communities, and businesses can help, too, by arranging recycling collections, or banning plastic bags. Governments are already starting to pass laws to limit things such as pollution, logging, and overfishing.

100 Planet Earth is the only home we have. It's also the only home for wild animals and plants. After us, it will be the home of future generations. What we do now will decide whether it ends up a messy, overheated planet, or one that's healthy and safe to live on.

Index

Entries in **bold** refer to main subject entries. Entries in *italics* refer to illustrations.